Your *Attitude* for Success

Choose your attitude for a better perspective on life and work

• second edition •

by **Alan Berg**

marketing & publishing, llc
ideas for when business isn't right

Your Attitude for Success
second edition
Paperback ISBN: 978-0-9889179-3-4
EPUB ISBN: 978-0-9889179-4-1
MOBI ISBN: 978-0-9889179-5-8
LCCN: 2013906200

Second Edition Published by
Left of Center Marketing & Publishing, LLC
Kendall Park, NJ © 2013
No part of this book may be used in any manner without written permision. For more information,
contact Alan Berg at **YourAttitude@AlanBerg.com**

Acknowledgements:
I would like to thank the following for their contributions to this book:
Editor: Carole Berg
Book Design: Tom Kato & Alan Berg
Cover Design: Ian Berg

Written and Printed in the USA

This book is dedicated to Carole, Adam & Ian

for inspiring me to laugh, to love

and to learn, every day.

Just in case I didn't tell you today...

I love you all.

Table of Contents

Introduction	9
Chapter 1 – Is your glass half-full?	11
Chapter 2 – Who's in charge here?	15
Chapter 3 – If I only had the time	19
Chapter 4 – Here we are at the crossroads	21
Chapter 5 – "Congratulations, today your training begins"	23
Chapter 6 – Put me in Coach	27
Chapter 7 – Here we are at the crossroads… again	29
Chapter 8 – What's your excuse?	33
Chapter 9 – The entrepreneurial spirit is alive and well	35
Chapter 10 – How did I get here?	39
Chapter 11 – Where do you find your inspiration?	43
Chapter 12 – If you're not in the game you can't score a goal	47
Chapter 13 – When I'm 6	51

Chapter 14 – It's bad mood day in Boston	53
Chapter 15 – It's your choice to be happy	57
Chapter 16 – Give more, get more	59
Chapter 17 – Someday Isle	63
Chapter 18 – Don't paint the house	67
Chapter 19 – How's your sales attitude?	71
Chapter 20 – Get in the Zone	75
Chapter 21 – Wonder Woman clapping her bracelets and making lightning	77
Chapter 22 – What's on your bucket list?	81
Chapter 23 – What I did for my birthday	85
Chapter 24 – A new chapter, a new challenge	87
Chapter 25 – The journey continues	91
From The Author	95
About The Author	99

Introduction

Thanks for picking up my book. I believe that the people who are achieving great things today don't necessarily have more money or more ideas than the rest of us. They just act on their ideas. The people not taking actions are often hampered by the fear of failure (or even the fear of success). Successful people accept that failure is a possibility and react to each failure as a learning opportunity; a speed bump, not a roadblock.

What is success? Not the dictionary definition, rather what does success mean to you? No one but you can define it, so what's your idea of success? I believe that success is achieved by taking the actions, big and small, necessary to better yourself personally and professionally.

Is success a function of money? Not necessarily. While there are people that measure their success by the size of their home or investment portfolio, there are others who use very different benchmarks. It's your success, it's your definition.

When I'm coaching, mentoring or consulting with a client I want them to see the possible roadblocks or land mines, but

I don't want it to stop them from pursuing their dreams. It's always better to walk into the minefield knowing where the mines are so you're better prepared to handle them. It's when you blindly rush ahead that you end up needlessly running into roadblocks.

Thanks for investing this time with me. Please enjoy the journey.

Chapter 1
Is your glass half-full?

Why do some people always find the worst in a situation when there's so much good to be found if only they'd look? We all carry a "victim card" in our pocket. Regardless of what's going on I choose not to pull mine out. That's my choice.

Isn't it our choice how to see every situation? Of course it is. While I consider myself a glass-half-full kind of guy, this isn't about being perpetually positive. I may be positive, but I'm also a realist. No Pollyanna here. You can't just click your red-sequined heels together and make everything alright. This is about understanding when you are and are not able to control your situation and then making the right choices and taking the right steps at that moment in time.

In the following chapters I'm going to share some stories from my own life and those of others, young and old, to help demonstrate this point. Please join me on this journey to a better perspective. I appreciate you coming along. After all, it's your choice.

It's easy to take a woe-is-me attitude when facing a challenge. It's so much easier to blame someone else, or something else for what's happening to you. It's the economy. It's the weather. It's a bad hair day (or bad hair decade - if you don't know me it would help here to see my photo on the book jacket). At the writing of this book we're in the middle of the worst housing downturn in our lifetime. During the housing bubble people were paying ridiculous prices for houses and now it's coming back to haunt them. They're upside down on their mortgages, owing a lot more than their houses are currently worth. But hold on, weren't there winners in that same bubble? For everyone that paid too much for their house there was someone who made that sale, someone who probably made a handsome profit on that house.

When did common sense go out of style?

My wife and I bought a two-bedroom townhouse, our first house, in 1986, at a time of very high interest rates. Out of necessity we took an adjustable rate mortgage. Interest rates were double digits back then so we needed an affordable option. What's interesting now is that, in looking back, we had to qualify, not only for the initial mortgage payment at the teaser rate, but also for the highest payment the adjustable rate mortgage could reset to. That makes sense now and it made sense back then. Of course we know that same logic wasn't applied in the recent bubble.

It's hard to feel sorry for someone who knowingly bought too much house, with a mortgage they could barely afford now, no less when the rate went up. Where was common sense? The bankers didn't have it. The buyers didn't have it.

When did a house become a short-term investment for the average buyer? When did a house become an investment that could only keep appreciating? I grew up with the understanding that a house was a roof over your head; a safe place to raise your family. In other words it's a home, not an investment.

Wealth is a number on a piece of paper.

A house, or a stock certificate, or your own product or service, only gets its true value when it changes hands. When someone pays money for it, that's what sets its value. If you're not selling your house, or stock, or service, the value you see is merely a number on a piece of paper or computer screen.

I can remember my older son calling me one day from his college internship. He was a business major in college and was working for a venture capital company as an accounting intern. He proudly exclaimed *"Dad, guess what I'm holding? It's a stock certificate worth $10 million."* I told him that he'd just learned a very important lesson. It's only worth $10 million if they sell it today. Tomorrow it could be worth $20 million, $5 million or nothing. It's just a number.

That paper stock certificate has no value until someone buys it. Ask anyone who watched their portfolio tank in the stock market slide as they watched their number go down. They never really had the higher value since they didn't sell at that time. Similarly they don't have today's number if they don't sell today.

I have a friend in Southern California who was lamenting to me one day about the value of her house. I asked her if she was selling the house and she said, *"No"*. I asked her if she was having trouble paying the mortgage and again she said, *"No"*. So I asked her why she was wasting time and energy worrying about something that was irrelevant now. It was a self-inflicted distraction.

What I've learned is that it's wrong to say that you're waiting for your house or portfolio to regain its value. You can't get back something you never had. You can only start from where you are today and try to make the right decisions going forward. OK, I'll get off my soapbox now.

Chapter 2
Who's in charge here?

Let's get back to the subject of blaming someone else or something else for our woes. That's easy. Taking responsibility is much harder. Taking responsibility means we're accountable to ourselves, heaven forbid! Of course, I'm kidding. We're always accountable to ourselves first. We're responsible for our feelings. You may have heard this quote from Eleanor Roosevelt from 1937:

"No one can make you feel inferior without your consent."

Well, no one can give you a lousy attitude without your consent, either. It's your choice how to act, or react, to what happens to and around you. I heard a great contemporary follow up to this from a colleague of mine:

"You can't help how people or things make you feel, but you can help how long you feel that way."

I love the concept here. It allows us to be affected by what happens to and around us, while still keeping us accountable for getting back up and moving forward. It's OK, and perfectly normal, to react to what's happening to and around us as long as we can learn to let it go and move on. If we still let it bother us weeks or months later that's no longer the other person, or that situation's fault. We're the one holding on to that feeling.

Let me give you a personal example. When I was 16, looking at colleges, my dad, at age 45, had a minor heart attack. I ended up staying home, in Queens (New York City), and commuting to a college in lower-Manhattan. It saved us money and also kept me close to my family. I could have resented that I didn't get to go away to college, as my friends had. I could have been bitter that I was denied the dorm experience. But I knew that I was where I needed to be at the time, for all of us.

Dad survived that heart attack but went on, years later, to have a triple bypass operation, a single bypass and a couple of stents (small "springs" placed inside an artery to keep it open). I'm happy to say that at age 81 he's still kicking, thanks to his 2 hip replacements along the way.

As a family we made changes to how and what we ate. Back in the 1970's a low-salt, low-fat diet was the guiding principle of healthy eating for a cardiac patient. We learned to eat bland food, not just my father, but the whole family.

Because of this, over thirty-five years later I still don't like very spicy foods.

My mother's family tends to live into their late 80's and 90's. Her father lived to 90, her mother to 93 and my great aunt passed away 2 months before her 98th birthday! Since my physique is more like my mother's father and my mother's brother than my father, I naturally expected that keeping slim and active, like them, would stave off the heart problems my father has experienced.

Ettu Mother?

Then, my mother, at age 65, found that her arteries were clogged, too. She went on over the following years to have 7 stents and then a quadruple bypass at age 74. Naturally, once she started having issues I tried to be more vigilant and keep myself fit and eat well. I thought I had been doing that already. Unfortunately eating well back in the 1970's and 1980's was not what we consider eating well today. It's hard to stay on target when the prevailing thinking of what is and isn't healthy keeps changing, isn't it?

Chapter 3
If I only had the time

One day I was watching my 2 sons at their Tae Kwon Do class and I was thinking *"That looks like fun; I wish I had the time to do it"*. I often had that thought because I had taken a karate class at a community college when I was in high school, but never went further. I'd always wanted to pick it up again and get a black belt. I didn't know what it meant to get a black belt, but I just knew that I wanted one, but I kept thinking *"I don't have the time for this"*.

Have you ever been there? You wanted to do something but you told yourself *"I don't have the time"*. We've all been there at one time or another.

Then, one day, something changed in my attitude and I had a man-in-the-mirror moment. I came to the realization that we never *have* time for anything in our lives. There are only 24 hours in a day and we're never getting any more, so every day we decide how to use ours. We prioritize family, work, sleep, spirituality, volunteering and recreation and allocate some of our limited time to each. Therefore I was never going to *have* time for Tae Kwon Do until I decided to *make* the time for it. It had to move up my priority list, and once it did, I started taking classes, at age 39.

After I made the decision to start classes I changed my perspective and, all of a sudden, I found the time to train in Tae Kwon Do three times a week... for 8 years! My clock and calendar didn't change. There was no genie that miraculously granted me any more time. It had always been my decision on how to use my 24 hours each day. I just changed my priorities.

We do this all the time without realizing it. A friend might call and tell you that they have an extra ticket to a concert, so you change your plans and go with them. You didn't get any more time; you just changed your priorities. You already had something to do, but you decided that going to the concert was a higher priority than whatever else you were going to be doing at that time. Those decisions are not conscious decisions to change your priorities, you just do it. You have the ability to change your priorities any time you want. Sometimes it's just easier than at other times.

Chapter 4
Here we are at the crossroads

Now that I was training 3 times a week in Tae Kwon Do I was really enjoying it. About 3 years later, at age 42, I was a few months from getting a first-degree black belt. I went to the doctor because I was getting winded more easily than I thought I should, especially being in great physical shape. It turned out that I was 90% blocked in 2 of my cardiac arteries. Left undetected this type of blockage could have easily led to a heart attack.

Clearing the blockage required inserting 5 stents into the two arteries. That was a wake-up call for me because I thought I was doing everything right. On paper I *was* doing everything right. I was exercising, eating well and I'd never smoked, so how could this happen?

So there I was, at the crossroads. I was probably in the best physical shape of my life, yet my "plumbing" was clogged. I knew that I had a choice to make. Do I crawl into my shell and stop pushing myself physically? Do I take the "why me?" attitude and pull out my "victim" card? Do I blame my parents or my genes for what happened to me? Or, do I accept that being in that good physical shape is probably what saved me from having a heart attack like my dad, who was overweight and sedentary when he had his heart attack at 45? I chose the latter. I took the attitude that I'd caught the problem; it had been taken care of, so let's move forward.

I recently heard that the first sign of heart disease for a large percentage of people is death. That's a sobering thought. Surely there had to be other signs. Other symptoms. Were the signs there? Were they ignored? We'll never know and I don't want to debate health care in this country here. I just know that medical science is advancing all the time so we can, and will do better.

Chapter 5

"Congratulations, today your training begins"

I got my black belt about 4 months after I had the 5 stents put in. It was a great day and a great feeling on many levels. It was a shared triumph for me, my family and my classmates. I was the only adult testing that day, along with 7 children, and I wasn't the tallest one testing (again, here it helps if you've seen me in person). It felt great. I was pumped. I was in the zone. I knew that getting my black belt was much sweeter than if I hadn't had the cardiac issues.

As part of the test and ceremony I had to write, and read out loud, an essay about what Tae Kwon Do meant to me. It was an emotional speech where I genuinely expressed that I felt Tae Kwon Do had saved my life. My voice cracked a few times and my eyes got a little watery, but I got through it.

Enjoy the journey

It also made me realize that getting a black belt is not a goal. Rather it's just a sign post along a journey. When I started Tae Kwon Do I was told that traditional martial arts is using your body to train your mind. Part of you is wondering what all the kicking and punching is for if you're training your mind. You don't understand it at first, but then one day, maybe weeks, months or years later, it clicks. It's hard to explain but once you get there, you just know.

As the Tae Kwon Do master was tying on my new black belt, embroidered in gold thread with my name on one end and the school's name on the other, he said *"Congratulations, today your training begins"*. My first thought was *"Huh? What were the last 3 1/2 years all about? Wasn't that training?"*

At that moment it was my choice how to react. I accepted that just as I eventually understood the whole "training your mind" thing, this too would eventually become clearer. Boy did it ever. What used to be acceptable kicking, punching and blocking movements were now met with minor adjustments and tweaks. When I did a block the master would move my hand ever so slightly, which at the time, could have seemed petty. That was the point. That was the training of your mind. My Tae Kwon Do master wanted to see our attitude and how we would react to the seemingly minor adjustments. Would we balk and say "Really? Was this 1/4 inch change really necessary?" Or would we say "Thank you, Sir"? It was my attitude and my choice of how to react.

Stop trying to be perfect

I remember him teaching us that we're not seeking perfection. It seemed counterintuitive. Wasn't perfection what we were trying to achieve? He explained that even if we could make a perfect kick, punch or block, we probably couldn't do it perfectly the very next time. If it were possible to achieve perfection wouldn't we be stepping backwards with the very next non-perfect action? There's no encore to perfection.

I meet lots of people who don't move forward at all because they're trying to be perfect. So instead, they do nothing and stay where they are. I often see this with someone who's making a new website, or writing a book, or painting a picture. It's never complete for them because it's not perfect. While I can certainly appreciate the desire to make it the best you can, perfection is too high of a bar to set for yourself. Make it the best you can make it today. Then tomorrow, make something that's better.

Striving for perfection is an illusion. What we're striving for is to be better than we were the last time. That's a brilliantly simple thought and a game-changer at the same time. We should always be moving forward. What a great lesson for life. Be a better parent, spouse, boss or mentor than you were yesteday. Be a better employee or teammate than you were yesterday.

We don't always have to have the big win to grow. Each incremental step forward is progress. Some are big, some are small. Sure, you want to have lofty dreams, but you can only reach them by taking one action at a time. Being better today than we were yesterday is something we can all achieve. Being better tomorrow is something we can all strive for today.

So launch that new website today and then improve upon it tomorrow. Write that new brochure and then make a better one next month. Design a new print or online ad and then make a better one for the next issue. Just do something. Don't get stuck waiting for it to be perfect.

I just read that there's a poster in Facebook's offices that says: *"Done is better than perfect"*. You can improve upon it tomorrow, just get something out there today that you can improve. If you keep it inside until it's perfect, it may never get out.

Chapter 6
Put me in Coach

I can remember Saturday morning meetings when I was selling Chrysler cars, before getting into advertising and media. The sales manager would go around the room asking each salesman how many cars he was going to sell that day. It was the equivalent of the pre-game locker room pep talk from a coach. Each rep would call out a number: 3 cars, 4 cars, 5 cars or more.

I was always number one or two in sales volume each month, as well as one of the top 50 Chrysler salesman in the country, but when he got to me I would say *"One! And when I'm done with that one I'm going to sell another one. And when that one's done I'm going to sell another one."* I had my eye on the first sale, not the 5th. I wasn't going to sell 5 cars to one person. I was going to sell one car to as many people as I could that day. You can't make the 5th sale until you've made the first one, so that was my focus. If I didn't give the first customer my full attention then I wouldn't make that sale. You don't win a race by jumping to the finish line. You have to run the whole race, every part of it, one leg at a time.

We've all experienced being in a store where the salesperson you're working with, instead of paying attention to you, is looking around the sales floor for a better prospect. You can tell that they're not giving you their full attention. How does that make you feel? Not very important, does it? I've always tried to live by a simple philosophy; if you don't like the way someone has treated you, don't treat others that way.

A word about goals

My uncle (also an author and speaker) recently presented me with a new perspective on goals. I've used the word a lot in my speaking, managing and consulting, but I never looked at it this way: Goals, by their nature, are self-limiting. They set an upper limit on what you're able to achieve.

So I started to think about my personal career in sales and I realized that I never really had goals. I just went about selling as much as I could, every day. With that philosophy I kepy increasing my sales, every year. I never really thought about it that way and I believe that many successful people think the same way. Thanks, Uncle Arnold.

Chapter 7
Here we are at the crossroads... again

About two years after I had my 5 stents put in I was a few months away from achieving my 2nd degree black. I was in even better physical shape than I had been for my 1st degree black belt testing. My wife and I attended our 27 year high school reunion (despite having a graduating class of over 1,200 we couldn't get enough interest for the 25th, go figure?). We were out on the dance floor but I was, again, getting winded more easily than I thought I should have. So I went to my cardiologist and told him about the times, like dancing, climbing stairs and pulling my suitcase through the airport, where I was getting winded. I had been doing Tae Kwon Do for about 5 years now and was in the best physical shape of my life. The natural insulation was off my 6 pack, so why was I getting winded at all?

Well, it turned out that one of my 5 stents was 90% blocked with scar tissue. How could this be? I was eating healthier than ever, choosing to eat more fish and organics. I was exercising vigorously 4 or 5 times a week. I was taking all of the cholesterol and blood pressure drugs he'd prescribed, like clockwork.

Where's that victim card?

How could this happen? I had a fleeting thought of pulling out my victim card, but that's not me. Regardless of how it happened we had to address it. The doctor did an angioplasty (a "balloon" to open the artery and a little Rotor-Rooter job to clear the scar tissue) on the clogged stent and I was back in business.

So, I found myself at the same crossroads again. Do I find a rock to crawl under or take my newly cleaned "pipes" and move forward? Again I decided that the problem was solved so I chose the latter and moved forward. Five months later, at age 44, I got my 2nd degree black belt. It was another proud day for me and my family. I even broke 30 boards in 36 seconds! If you had told me when I was 20 that I would get a 2nd degree black belt when I was 44, I would have said that you were nuts. Then again if you had told me when I was 20 that I would be an author, a professional speaker and marketing expert I probably would have thought you to be just as crazy. Perspective is a wonderful thing.

I stopped Tae Kwon Do a couple of years later when I got a couple of bulging discs in my back doing a particularly vigorous kick. It was very humbling. I was at the peak of my physical condition. I'd been training for 8 years, going to classes 3 times each week and I was only about 6 months away from earning a 3rd degree black belt. Remember that Tae Kwon Do is something I told myself I didn't have the time to do before I started, eight years earlier. I didn't find the time for it. First I made it my priority, and then as it became part of my life, it became somewhat of a necessity.

Who's to blame here?

After months of physical therapy my back was better but I came to the realization that I couldn't do Tae Kwon Do any more. It wasn't the doctor that said it. It wasn't the physical therapist. It was me being afraid that I would hurt my back again doing Tae Kwon Do. With that fear in my head, *I was limiting myself, and I knew it.* I knew that if I went into class afraid I would get hurt then it was much more likely that I would. This fear was amplified by the intensity of my training. So I quickly came to accept that I had a good run, going farther than I ever thought I would in martial arts and I came to peace with not going back.

I thought it would be hard to walk away after going 3 times per week for 8 years. It was surprisingly easy because I had taken full responsibility for the decision. I sometimes feel guilty that I don't feel guilty about stopping my training. It would have been easier to blame the doctor or therapist but I knew it was *me* placing the limitation on *myself*. I really loved my Tae Kwon Do training. To this day it surprises me how I've never looked back, but it's the power of taking responsibility for my decision.

Chapter 8
What's your excuse?

Given my medical history I knew I still needed to exercise so I took a different approach. I remembered a story my father had told me back in the 1970's after his heart attack. He had been going to a cardiac support group and he told me about a man he met who was a runner. He ran every day, rain or shine. He'd been running the morning of their support group meeting which had been a particularly cold, rainy, wintery day in New York. My father asked him why he went running that day, given the nasty weather. The man told him that he ran every day because *"if he found an excuse not to run today he would find an excuse not to run when it was 75 and sunny"*.

Every day means every day, no excuses.

How wonderfully simple that philosophy was, and is. So, I decided that I would exercise every day. I exercise inside so I don't have to deal with the wide range of weather in the northeast or when I travel. It reduces the possible excuses for not doing so. I figured that exercising would be like giving me a stress-test every day so I would ensure that if there *was* a problem, I would catch it early.

I was fanatical at first; beating myself up if I missed even one day. I became "that guy". Do you know someone like that? They just have to go to the gym every day. They'll blow off other opportunities so they don't miss even one day. Then I came to the realization that I probably skip less days exercising each month than most people get to the gym. Now I try to exercise every day but if I miss a day, or if I have an early presentation or flight, I don't sweat it. I know I'll be exercising tomorrow.

Am I hitting a nerve here? Are you paying your gym membership every month but you hardly ever go? Is that treadmill or bike acting as a clothes hanger or dust collector? At one time you decided that a gym membership or piece of exercise equipment was a good idea. You were right, so what happened? It's your 24 hours each day to prioritize.

What's more important in your day than your physical health? I know, first-hand, that if you don't have your health you're not much good to your family or work. It's your choice how to use your 24 hours. Is it time to make a better choice? That's for each of us to decide every day.

Chapter 9
The entrepreneurial spirit is alive and well

Do you own your own business? There's a really good chance if you're reading this book that you do now, at some time in your life you did or maybe you're planning to do so in the future. At some point you made the decision, conscious or not, to start or buy a business.

The entrepreneurial spirit is a wonderful thing. It's an attitude that you have something to offer others, something valuable enough that you want to share it. You have a skill and a passion that drew you into wanting to share that with others... and hopefully make some money along the way. You didn't think about failure when you started your business, you planned to succeed.

Are you an accidental businessperson? You have a skill, passion or talent and, one day, someone offered to pay you for your product or service. Then someone else did and another and, well, then you were in business.

And now you're in business

You may not have realized you were going into business at the time, and you certainly didn't ask for the responsibilities that come along with it (expenses, payroll, rent, insurance, headaches, sleepless nights, etc.), but you found yourself in business. I applaud you for that. I understand that spirit. I've had a few of my own businesses starting from when I was a teenager with a rock and roll band. Then a friend and I had the idea to photograph and videotape people's houses and valuables to have a visual record for insurance purposes. Then I had a small burglar alarm company.

More recently my wife and I published two WeddingPages magazines, in New Jersey and the Hudson Valley in NY. We sold those magazine franchises back to WeddingPages. They wanted me to come work for them as a Regional Sales Director, managing their sales reps in the northeast. Shortly thereafter that company was purchased by The Knot. I worked there for 11 years, most of them as a Vice President, overseeing the local sales team, sales operations and training. Once again I find myself self-employed, this time as an author, professional speaker, coach and marketing consultant.

Starting a business is scary. Some of you did it because you wanted to. Some because you couldn't find the job you really wanted so you created it. Down economies often see a boon in startups. Most of the jobs created in this country come from small businesses. Some people are looking for the American dream while others are looking for something else or something new. Kudos to you for taking that leap.

Don't fear success

When I was researching for my presentation *"Fearless - conquering the new reality"* I came across many articles that talk about how some people actually fear success. They're afraid of what success might do to change their status-quo. How it might alter their relationships or put additional pressures on them. So they actually sabotage their own success and upward mobility to avoid the unknown. It's the same unknown that intrigues others that scares them.

Are you afraid of success? Are you putting off actions that could move your life or business ahead because you fear the unknown? Recognizing that is a very important first step. Taking the first action towards whatever you seek is the next important step.

Chapter 10
How did I get here?

I have the good fortune now of doing what I love and loving what I do. My older son recently told my wife that he wanted to *"love his job as much as Dad loves his"*. Yeah, it made us both tear up a little.

It hasn't always been this way for me. If I hadn't hated the job I had before getting into wedding media, I wouldn't be where I am now. I took a position that ended up being very different from what I had expected. Was it my fault? Did the company misrepresent the position? It didn't matter; I dreaded going to work every day. To compound the situation I was working 12 hour days, our son was turning 3, my wife was expecting our second child and I was hardly ever home.

The job challenged my ethics and values. Even though I hated the job I produced much more than they had expected when I was hired. My parents had always instilled in me that if you take a job you should always do it the best you can. If you don't like the job... leave and find something else, but never do a bad job. So I toiled away every day, doing a very good job, but hating every minute. The company was thrilled. I was miserable.

Then one day a friend called to tell me he'd bought the WeddingPages magazine for New Jersey. He didn't want a partner, he wanted me to come and sell print advertising for him. Common sense and responsibility said I shouldn't do it. It was a commission-only sales position for a new business. I would have to give back my company car, buy a car, and arrange for health insurance, all for the unknown of this new sales job. I leapt at the opportunity.

A leap of faith

On paper it looked like a foolish and irresponsible thing to do. I would be giving up a good-paying job, with a pregnant wife, to go on straight commission (no salary, no draw, and no guarantee). When I gave my two-week's notice, my manager showed me how much money I was making, for me and for them. At the tender age of thirty it was my first epiphany that life is not about the money. I was making the money, but I was miserable. In retrospect it's fortunate for me that I did hate that job. Had I loved it I might have stayed and missed out on the journey that led me here to a career I thoroughly enjoy.

Serendipity or fate?

Life is funny that way. You often don't know where you're going. But when you get there you can look back and see how you were presented with opportunities each step along the way. Some opportunities you took and some you passed on. Every time it was your choice. Each of those choices led you to the next step. I often tell my sons that it's OK to pass on an opportunity as that's still making a choice. What's unfortunate is when you didn't see the opportunity at all and therefore you never had the chance to even make a choice.

Opportunities are around us all the time. If we keep our eyes open we'll see them. When your next opportunity presents itself will you have the strength to make the decision or will you let someone else decide for you? It's easier to let someone else decide. That lets you off the hook. You can then point your finger at someone else if you're not happy with the outcome or not performing well. It's easier, but it's not as satisfying as owning the decision.

If you've never had the opportunity to read or see Steve Jobs' commencement address to the graduating class of Stanford University, in 2005, please look it up online. It's referred to as the "connecting the dots" speech, as he talks about how you can't connect the dots in life looking forward. You can only look back and see how one thing led to another.

Chapter 11
Where do you find your inspiration?

Finding inspiration is easy. It's all around us. I met a young lady at a National Speakers Association (the leading organization for professional speakers where I'm proud to be a member) meeting in New Orleans. She left a six- figure job to pursue a career as a professional speaker. What surprised me was the story of how she got there. She got pregnant in high school at age 15. She was fortunate that her family supported her instead of disowning her as many families might have done. Rather than having to drop out of school and ending up on welfare, as so many in that situation do, she finished High school, got a full scholarship to college and went on to get her masters degree and a well-paying corporate job. She's had some rough patches but she's still married to the father of her daughter from High school and now has a successful speaking business of her own.

It was an amazing story. We were sitting next to each other at dinner, talking about lots of different things, when she started a sentence with *"I really haven't had it that bad in life..."* and before she could go on I stopped her. It amazed me that someone who had been through what she had, could have the attitude that she hasn't had it that rough. I can't imagine having gone through what she did and thinking that I hadn't had it rough. Now that's perspective. It was her attitude, her choice.

But it's only a yellow rubber bracelet

There are countless stories and inspiration around us every day. Until the recent Lance Armstrong scandal, I used to wear a yellow "Livestrong" bracelet (his cancer charity) to remind me that every day people wake up to cancer and other personal challenges, things most of us would find unimaginable. I realize that many people could perceive the heart issues I've been through as unimaginable but things always look different through our own eyes.

Putting on the yellow bracelet each morning was my daily dose of perspective. It was my affirmation that today is going to be a good day. I even kept a supply of them on hand for when one broke. It had gotten that I felt naked without it.

My wife and I decided that while the cause was still worthy, the symbolism of supporting the man behind it was not. I'm looking for my new daily visual.

Make it your choice

Life deals us choice cards all the time. It's our attitude and our choice how to react. As I said before, I believe that you need to keep your eyes open to the opportunities in life and then, hopefully, have the strength and wisdom to make a choice for yourself. My hope is that you will always see the opportunities that are around you all the time.

My older son was recently having a career crisis and I saw that he was trying to plan five steps ahead. I told him not to worry that far out. Figure out what you want to do next and then keep your eyes open to the opportunities. As I write this he's about to start a new position in his company and he's very excited about it. Who knows where this will lead? We don't and that's what's exciting. We don't have to have every step pre-planned. The magic happens when we allow ourselves to be open to seeing the opportunities and possibilities.

Chapter 12

If you're not in the game you can't score a goal

I can remember driving in New Jersey back in the early 1990's selling ads in the WeddingPages magazine, a time I like to refer to as B.I. (before the Internet). This was the franchise that my friend had bought and, at the time, I was his only salesman. I regularly logged 100 to 200 miles a day cold-calling and visiting clients. I was driving down a local street I had never been on and I saw a new bridal shop. My natural instinct was to stop in and cold-call them. That was the right thing to do. But something was different that day. I just didn't feel like making a cold-call.

I can't remember what else had happened that day. Maybe I'd been on other calls that didn't go so well. Maybe the weather was too nice and I didn't want to go inside. Maybe I was just tired. I honestly don't remember, but I vividly remember not wanting to stop, so I kept driving. I got about 4 blocks down the road and I pulled over. I literally turned the rear view mirror around and looked at myself. As I write this I can still see my eyes in the mirror. I said, if you'll pardon the expression, *"Schmuck! If you don't stop in you have absolutely no chance of making a sale. If you do, you're at least in the game. So what's it going to be?"*

Working without a net (safety net that is)

Remember that I was on straight commission, no salary or benefits. My family was depending on me. I had two young sons and a stay-at-home wife. We lived on my commissions. There was no good reason *not* to stop in.

So, there I was, at another one of life's crossroads. Have you ever been there? You knew what you needed to do but you just didn't feel like making the effort. You just couldn't get yourself to take that action so you put it off for a while or maybe forever. What did I do? I drove around the block and stopped in.

The big win wasn't the sale

I can't remember if I made the sale, but that wasn't my big win that day. Changing my attitude was the big win.

Overcoming whatever was stopping me at that moment was the big win. I realized that I was behind the wheel, literally and figuratively. We're not puppets with someone else pulling the strings, we control our actions. We control our attitude.

Do the hard parts first

So the next time you find yourself at that crossroads dig deep to find the strength to do what you know you should. I used to tell my sons to do the hardest part of their homework first. They always wanted to do the easy parts and put off the harder assignments until later. I explained to them that they should do the hard parts while they were more energetic and save the easier things for when they were more tired. Putting off the hard things until you're tired will just make them seem even more onerous.

I can recall having a Post-it note on my desk with the name and phone number of an upset customer whom I needed to call. The longer I put off making that call (so I wouldn't have to get yelled at) the larger that Post-it note seemed to get. My anticipation of what might happen on that call was keeping me from making it. Of course the longer I waited to call, the angrier that customer was going to be, so I was only making it worse for myself.

However if I made the call right away I could get it done and off my desk. The rest of the day I wouldn't have to stare at it, watching it appear to get larger and larger. Eventually I learned to make the difficult calls as quickly as possible to the benefit of both the customer and myself. It's like ripping off a Band-Aid.

Chapter 13
When I'm 6

Life is full of seminal moments. I can remember when my older son was 5 and learning to ride a bike. I wanted to take off his training wheels because he seemed to be doing so well. His balance was really good and the training wheels were hardly touching the ground as he was riding. But every time I tried to take them off he would tell me *"Daddy, I can't ride a two wheeler now, I'm only 5. When I'm 6 I'll be able to ride a two-wheeler."*

No matter how much encouragement I gave him he told me the same thing: *"When I'm 6 I'll be able to ride a two-wheeler."* Sure enough, on the morning he turned 6 I took off his training wheels and he rode like he'd been riding for years. He had convinced himself that he couldn't ride a two-wheeler until he was 6 and therefore he wouldn't even try. It was a self-imposed limitation. The difference is that he vocalized his self-limitation and what it would take for him to be able to move forward, then, when that self-imposed barrier was removed, he lived up to it and moved forward.

In my son's case he had verbalized his self-limitation at the tender age of 5. As adults we're not always able to see when we're getting in our own way. We do it to ourselves all the time and don't even know it. The difference is that we often find it easier to put a new limitation in our way when the first one is removed, rather than moving forward.

Have you been putting off making a new website because of one excuse after another? Have you been talking about losing weight or starting an exercise program, but not taking any steps to achieve it? Have you talked about writing a book but you haven't put any words down on a page? What limitations are you putting on yourself? What roadblocks are you putting in your own way that are unnecessary? What roadblocks are you imagining that are in your power to remove, if you really want to?

Chapter 14
It's bad mood day in Boston

When I was a Regional Sales Director at The Knot, I had a sales rep who called me late one morning, lamenting about how everyone she had called so far that day was in a bad mood. I let her go on about this for a few minutes as she recounted story after story of how poorly her sales calls went that morning.

When she had finished venting I reassured her that I'd checked my calendar and it wasn't "bad mood day in Boston". I also reassured her that her clients and prospects weren't calling each other and plotting to be in a bad mood if she called them. I told her that I believe the world is a mirror. You get what you give. If you project negativity the other person will sense it and you'll often get back negativity. I felt that it was very likely that *she* was the one in the bad mood and her prospects were picking up on it.

She, of course, disagreed with me. She thought she was in a fine mood. So I told her that, lucky for her, I knew exactly what she needed to do. She, like most of our local sales reps worked from a home office. I told her that what she really needed was to leave her office, right now, for at least an hour, by the clock. Not forty-seven minutes, a full hour. Take a walk, go get lunch, go to the gym… whatever, just get out of her house for an hour.

She was surprised at my direction, but she agreed to do it. I called her back late that afternoon and asked how the rest of her day was going. She said it was *"Terrific!"* She had made three sales after coming back home. She was amazed at how much better of a mood her prospects seemed to be in compared to the morning. It wasn't her prospects that had the issue at all. *She* was the one that needed the "attitude adjustment". She needed a change of scenery to help facilitate her attitude change.

Surround yourself with positive voices

It's easy for your attitude to get off track, especially when you work alone from home. The key is to surround yourself with positive voices and influences. Who do you know that just talking to them or being around them puts you in a better mood? We all know people like that. I don't mean the Pollyanna's who are little Miss Sunshine all the time to the point where it's almost fake. I mean those people who exude that certain something that just makes you want to be a better you. I'm sure your mind immediately went to a special person in your life.

On the other hand, we also all know people that just being around them sucks the life out of you. You dread seeing them or calling them because you know it's going to drain your energy. They can turn a sunny-day disposition into a black cloud. You feel bad avoiding them but you know that your personal outlook is better off for it. Can you change their attitude? Probably not because it's not yours to change, it's theirs. What you can change is if, or how long, you let them affect *your* attitude.

Chapter 15
It's your choice to be happy

I was in the NY City offices of The Knot a few years ago and it was one of those days that seemed to have a dark cloud over it. The energy level in the office, usually a vibrant place, seemed to be low. Everyone to whom I said *"Hi, how are you?"* seemed to grunt their answer. I walked into the office of a local project manager and I said *"How 'ya doing, Julie?"* She said with a sigh *"It's one of those days"*. Her answer had no energy in it either. It all struck me as strange and out of character for her and the office.

Then she said *"How are you doing, Alan?"* I thought about it for a second and something clicked in me. I don't know why but I replied with a smile *"I'm choosing to be happy for the rest of the day. Would you like to join me?"* A huge smile came across her face and she said *"Sure!"* but her reply now had feeling and was uplifting. So we literally shook hands in agreement and then I left her office, with both of us smiling.

Amazingly the black cloud felt like it had lifted. That same office, which only minutes before appeared to be lifeless, suddenly appeared vibrant again. I walked around with a smile on my face the rest of the day. I can only guess that it was me that had been choosing to see the black cloud in the office that day. I know that I don't have the power to change the attitude of a whole office in a few minutes, with one sentence. It had to be me. It had been my choice to first see the negative and now to see the positive.

Chapter 16
Give more, get more

It's likely that now, or at some point in your career, you've been a member of at least one trade association, local networking group, club, church group or community organization. You may even be a member of more than one association or group. If you've been a member for a few years or more, you've probably learned that the more you give to the group, the more you'll get in return. But you have to *give unselfishly*. If you're only seen to give because you're expecting quid pro quo, something in return, then others will not give as willingly to you. However, when you give without expecting anything in return, you always get back much, much more.

Here's a less well known Eleanor Roosevelt quote, also from 1937: *"The most important thing in any relationship is not what you get but what you give."*

As I find myself self-employed again I'm amazed and touched by the support of so many people I've met through my years in the wedding industry. I've always been a big supporter of local businesses and trade associations and now that support is coming back around to me, without my asking. It's truly humbling.

How can I help you?

As a member of the National Speakers Association (the other NSA), the leading organization for professional speakers, our unofficial motto is *"How can I help you?"* This permeates from the newest member to the most senior, experienced speaker. I can remember going to my second NSA conference and attending a session for new members. We were in a room with large round tables. At each one was a long-time NSA member. Everyone at my table was freely sharing ideas and conversation. We were talking about business, life and family. It was a very relaxed, casual atmosphere. I introduced myself to the long-time member at my table, a grandfatherly looking gentleman named Howard, who had been generously sharing ideas and advice with each of us.

When I asked about him, he very casually said he was Howard Putnam, former CEO of Southwest Airlines. Here was this major corporation CEO chatting with me and the other newbies at our table. He was unselfishly giving of his time and knowledge, offering information and ideas, never asking us for anything. This has inspired me to give of myself, both to the NSA as well as to my friends, family, colleagues, clients and the many trade associations I work with. I always seem to get much more when I give while asking for nothing. It's also much more satisfying to have others offer their assistance when you haven't asked. It shows that they genuinely care about your success, not just their own.

◇ ◇ ◻ ◇ ◇

Chapter 17
Someday Isle

So what can you do to change your attitude? First you have to *realize and accept that your attitude is yours to choose.* If you don't accept that then you can't make any progress.

Next you have to listen to your own language. Are you speaking like a victim or are you sounding like you're in control? Do you speak about what "I" can do? Or do you talk about what *"they're doing to me"*? Do you tell yourself *"I could do that if only something else would happen, or someone else would do something"*?

Start focusing on the positive. Think about what you want to achieve and make a plan to get there. Plan to succeed, don't live in the land of *"What if..."*

I remember hearing, years ago, about people who live on *Someday Isle*. You know *"Someday I'll (Isle) write that book"* or *"Someday I'll go to Ireland"* or *"Someday I'll go skydiving"*.

I can't remember who first said but if you do an online search you'll find many links, with many sources.

For me, Someday Isle is when you talk about and think about the places you'll go and the things you'll do... someday, but you never take any real action. You don't take any tangible steps towards actually being able to achieve those goals. It doesn't stop you from talking about them, but you have no chance of achieving them because the only effort you give them is lip-service.

Where did I find the time?

Often taking the first step is the hardest. I kept telling myself that I didn't have the time to take Tae Kwon Do classes, but once I took that first step I "miraculously" had the time to go three days a week, for 8 years. I always had the time; I just had to rearrange my priorities.

When I published my first book, *"If your website was an employee, would you fire it?"*, I had so many people say to me *"I've been wanting to write a book, how did you do it?"*. I told them that I did it one word at a time. I set myself a deadline and I started writing. As it was my first book I didn't really understand the timeline so I missed my self-imposed deadline, but only by a couple of months. Most of the people who said that to me are still waiting to get started. As you well know I've now written my second book (the one you're reading is the second edition of that book), I've published the second edition of my website book and I've published a mini-book based upon the story in the next chapter. By the time you're reading this I've probably already started on book three.

Last year I spoke in Canada, Ireland and Mexico, all of which I'll be back speaking in again this year. Later this year I'm scheduled to speak in Bali and possibly, Australia. It's a very humbling and exciting time. Anything is possible.

What are you waiting for?

What have you been putting off personally or professionally? Where have you been planning to go? What business changes have you been talking about? What self-imposing road-blocks are you putting in your own way, blocking your success personally, in your business, or both?

Getting a black belt and writing a book were two of my *Someday Isle's*. By now you all know about my second degree black belt and this is my second book, so believe me when I say that Someday Isle is a state of mind that you, too, can surpass. You just need to take the first step, which will lead to the next step and so on.

Chapter 18
Don't paint the house

An associate of mine bought a house la couple of years ago. I was very proud of her. She's a single Mom and it was a great way for her and her then 4 year old daughter to take a step forward. She'd been complaining for months that she needed to paint the house, but she didn't have the time.

The problem was that she was trying to figure out when she would have time to paint the whole house. It was too big of a job to comprehend so, like many of us, she ended up doing nothing, except complaining about how she needed to paint the house. She never started the job. She didn't buy the paint or brushes. She didn't pick the colors.

So, one day I told her *"Don't paint the house."* She replied *"But the house needs to be painted"*. I said *"You don't have time to paint the house"*. She said *"Yeah, that's the problem."* So I asked her, *"Can you paint a wall this weekend?"*

She sounded puzzled. I asked her again, *"Can you paint one wall, in one room, this weekend?"* Then she started to tell me about how she needed to patch and plaster and she didn't have a ladder tall enough for the cathedral ceiling. So I went online to a big box home improvement store's site and sent her a link to an edging pad painter that she could use with a broomstick or long pole, without a ladder, and reach the high parts of the wall.

Then I asked her *"Now, can you patch, plaster and paint one wall, in one room, this weekend?"* She said *"Yes"*. I said, OK, paint one wall this weekend and then try to paint another one or two during the week. By next weekend a whole room will be done. Had she painted even one wall in each room every week since she bought the house, the whole house would have been painted already.

Break it down

Sometimes you just need to break your project down into more manageable goals. You never really paint a whole house at once; you always paint one area at a time. You can apply that same outlook to almost any task.

If you're thinking you need a new website, don't think of it as one task, it's many small tasks. First you need to decide what your site is going to be and who it's for. Reading my book *"If your website was an employee, would you fire it?"* will help you with this part. Next you need to choose a company to do the site. Then you need to decide which pages you're going to include. Then what content will be on each page, and so on.

If you're looking to make changes to your business (rebranding, raising prices. adding new products or services, expanding into a new area, etc.) break it down into smaller, more manageable projects. When you can see the smaller tasks you'll be more motivated to get started. When you look at one, huge task, you often get paralyzed and do nothing.

Shorten your to-do list

I recently erased the large white-board in my office. There were way too many projects on there, some of which I'd probably never get to doing. What usually happens is that as we start doing some of our projects we move our businesses to a new place. The things that are left on our lists may not be appropriate for where we are today. A good piece of advice is to only keep 3 or 4 things on your list. Then, as you cross them off, make a new list of what's important to you where you are today.

So, what is it you've been putting off? What project, task or goal seems too large and is paralyzing from getting started? This isn't just about professional goals. Are you trying to quit smoking, lose weight or learn a new language?

What self-imposing road-blocks are you putting in your own way to success personally, in your business, or both? You can move those roadblocks, but first you have see them and accept that they're yours to move, if you really want to.

Today list vs. To-do list

When I refer to my To-do list it's actually the big-picture things I'm working on. My list is comprised of things like writing a book, producing new products (DVDs, Audio CDs, etc.), learning a new language (I have Rosetta Stone Spanish Edition loaded on my laptop and I'm studying on my many flights). That's my to-do list.

We all also have a "Today list", the things we need to get done today. The problem that many of us run into is when our Today list prevents us from getting to our To-do list. That happens very easily as we have to put out the fires that are burning today. Even firemen know that you have to do preventative measures to stop new fires from breaking out. What you need to do is put a small piece of your To-do list on your Today list. It doesn't have to be huge, but do something. If you don't then you'll never get to finish those big-picture items.

Chapter 19

How's your sales attitude?

In these uncertain economic times I know that many of you are coming up against price-conscious shoppers. For many of you it's frustrating or worse. It affects how you interact with that prospect, or customer, from that point forward. I actually don't think it's fully a reflection of a weak economy. We're all consumers and we all act the same way when we're buying something new. When we don't know what else to ask, we ask how much it costs. It's the one, common denominator for everyone. So, if we all do it, we should accept that our customers are going to do it as well. We need to frame our attitude for how we react to these situations.

So, how do you feel when you come up against price shopping customers? Do you feel confident in the value of your services, or do you feel out of control? What's your first thought when you speak to a price-shopper? Is it one of disgust *"Oh great, another price shopper"*? Or is it the positive way I choose to react to price shoppers? My first thought is *"Thank you. Thanks for putting me on your list of possible choices."* My feeling is that if they aren't shopping me for price then I may not have had any shot at all of getting their business at all.

They still haven't found what they're looking for

You're probably thinking that all they want is a better price. I'm thinking that *if they were completely satisfied* with what they had seen and heard at other vendors in my industry, including price, then why didn't they already book someone else? Something is still missing and it's not necessarily a better price. We don't keep shopping when we find everything we want.

If you're a service business, which many of you reading this book are, then price is only one of many factors. Actually, everyone is in the service business. You win or lose on service. Price only matters after all of her other needs are satisfied. Let's face it, if you're not available on the date they need you then price doesn't matter. If you don't do the style of work that they want (music, food, photos, flowers, painting, dog walking or whatever you do), then price doesn't matter. If they don't like the way your offices look, the way you dress or your personality, then price doesn't matter. If they're afraid that you won't or can't deliver the services they want or that you won't have a backup plan if something goes wrong, then price doesn't matter. And most of all, if they don't like your attitude, then price doesn't matter.

They're shopping for a complete experience.

They have to like you and trust that you'll be able to fulfill not only their technical needs, but also their emotional ones. Then, only after those needs are satisfied, does price matter. Yes, most purchases have an emotional component to the decision making, not just weddings and events. Prospects have and will spend more with a competitor of yours to satisfy their needs, whether you know it or not.

I know a couple of young women who were shopping for their wedding dresses and they told me that they didn't buy them at the cheapest place in town. They even acknowledged that the price and selection were better at other stores, but they didn't like the customer experience at the cheaper stores. They spent more for their dresses than they could have and they were completely happy with their decisions. They didn't specifically think about it that way, but that was the end result. They bought from people they liked and trusted and paid more for the privilege.

They were the inspiration for my presentation: *"Creating an Exceptional Customer Experience"*. We all want a better experience, not just the right price. The right experience beats a lower price most of the time.

We've all done this and most of the time it's not a conscious choice, it's a gut feeling. If you need a plumber, do you want the cheapest one, regardless of the quality of his work? Of course not. If you have any trepidation that someone won't or can't deliver, or you don't like the way they communicate with you in person, on the phone or in an email, you'll look elsewhere, even if it means paying more.

There's only one you

You don't always have to beat the price they've gotten elsewhere to get the sale. *If you're a service business then they can't get what makes you different anywhere else; and that's you and your team.* Even if you're in a product-based business it's usually the customer experience that wins you a sale. So when you get the next price shopper, first understand that you're now in the game and be happy about that. Next, understand that they often ask about price first because they doesn't know what else to ask. Then get to the real root of what they're looking for because they haven't found it yet.

Chapter 20
Get in the Zone

No one can put limitations on you. You do that to yourself or accept the limitations others impose upon you. You decide what you're capable of, or not. Others can try to limit you with their negative talk, but ultimately you control whether or not to buy into their words. Likewise, you decide whether to buy into the pep-talk and encouragement of your supporters.

Can you recall being in "the Zone"? You know, that feeling that you're absolutely sure you're going to succeed. Maybe it was in sports, in your business or in your personal life. It's that feeling of confidence that you exude and others pick up on it. They want to be around you when you're in the Zone, hoping it will rub off on them. You want to be around others when they're in the Zone. It's contagious. Remember when I wrote earlier about wanting to be around certain people because they make you feel better about yourself? Those are often people who are in the Zone.

You see it when a sports team gets the upper hand in a game. The team gains a momentum that's almost unstoppable. The converse of that is the hopeless feeling the other team gets. No matter what little gains they may make, they just can't seem to pull it together. Both feelings are contagious.

Have you been there? I'm sure you have. We all have. I'm not talking about cockiness. I'm talking about confidence, positive attitude and focus. It sure beats fear, trepidation and chaos. The thing with the *Zone* is that you can't just *will* yourself into it. There's no switch you can use to turn it on and off. Getting in the *Zone* is a result of your actions and reactions to what's happening right now around you. You can increase your chances by keeping an open mind and looking for the opportunities around you. If you're not looking, or worse, you live with blinders on, you're making it unlikely that you'll get in the *Zone*. Open your eyes to the endless possibilities around you. They are there if you'll allow yourself to see them.

Chapter 21

Wonder Woman clapping her bracelets and making lightning

I had a sales rep that called me one day and said that she could get a sale for a full page ad in our magazine if we matched the price they had gotten from a local competitor. I told her that I believed she could get the sale without matching the price. He had indicated to her that he wanted to advertise with us, but he was using the competitor's lower price as a negotiating tool.

I reminded her of a couple of things. First, it's his right to ask for a better price and our right to say Yes, or No. Next I reminded her that we don't sell advertising. She wasn't selling square inches on a page; she was selling access to our audience, something the competitor couldn't give him, at any price. I told her to ask him which brides he wanted to see his ad, the ones who read the other magazine or the ones who read ours? If he wanted the brides who read the other magazine he should buy their ad, at their price. However, if he wanted the brides who read our magazine, he had to buy our ad from her and pay our price. It wasn't an apples to apples comparison. It may have been the same size ad on the same size page, but the audience wasn't the same, therefore we didn't have to match the price. She was trying to work me over when she should have been showing him real the value of what she was selling.

Trust yourself

I convinced her that she could get the sale without lowering the price and gave her the tools to justify the value. After all, if she still had doubts then she wouldn't be able to hold her ground. I told her to trust me and go back to the customer. She called me a half-hour later, absolutely giddy that she had gotten the sale, at our price.

I asked her how she felt and she said *"Great!"* I asked her *"Do you feel strong?"* She said *"Yes!"* I asked *"Do you feel empowered?"* She emphatically said *"Yes!"* Then I asked her *"Do you feel like Wonder Woman clapping your bracelets together and making lightning?"* and she enthusiastically said *"Yes!"*.

I told her that she needs to hang up with me right now. She was puzzled and asked *"Why?"* I said *"The way you feel right now, you're unstoppable. You're in the Zone. Your attitude is one of confidence and you need to be talking to customers now, not to me."* So she hung up and I emailed her a Wonder Woman graphic. I told her to print it out and put it on her wall to remind her of how she felt right now. I said that any time she felt low on confidence she should look at this graphic, remember how she feels right now, clap her bracelets together and feel the power. It's in all of us, all the time, waiting for us to bring it out.

Show me a picture

Can you find a visual that inspires you? I'm sure you can. The beauty here is that each of us will have a different visual and that's exactly the point. One person's inspiration is merely a photo or drawing to someone else. The inspiration is within you all the time. Sometimes we just let it get clouded by other things going on around us at the time. Find yourself a visual that helps you to clear the clouds whenever you're having trouble being at your best.

◇ ◊ ◻ ◊ ◇

Chapter 22

What's on your bucket list?

Long before the movie *"The Bucket List",* with Jack Nicholson and Morgan Freeman, I had my own, unwritten list of things I wanted to do in my lifetime. I used to call it "50 things I want to do before I die" even though it was rarely more than a handful of thoughts. Getting a black belt was one of them, but I really didn't know what that meant when I put it on my list. Once I got my first degree black belt I was in a different mindset about what getting a black belt meant. It wasn't a destination. It wasn't the end of a road. It was merely a mile-marker along a personal journey. Your perspective often changes once you reach a milestone. The view is different from there.

In traditional martial arts there are only 2 belts, white and black. The colored belts are a modern invention, a way to show progress to a sometimes shallow society that needs validation, and quite frankly, to commercialize the industry... to make money. Any of you who have kids doing martial arts know that with every new belt comes a bill.

Fade to white

In traditional martial arts the belief is that you start with a white belt and train hard for many years. When you've trained long and hard enough you'll eventually earn your black belt. Once you get a black belt you'll have that same black belt for the rest of your life, unlike me getting a new belt with every level of black belt. If you're diligent enough, and fortunate enough, to continue training in that martial art your whole life, eventually your black belt would be so old and well-worn it would fade back to white, completing the full circle. This is a form of the Yin and Yang. Reflect on this for a moment. It's a pretty cool thought and very profound.

A clean bill of health... or is it?

About 5 years ago I had my annual stress test and passed with flying colors. I was running like the wind, at a very steep incline, on the treadmill in the doctor's office and the scans showed my "pipes" to be clean. That September, only three months later, I noticed in my daily exercise that I had to cut back one level, first occasionally, then every day. I went to my doctor and he said that doing another stress test probably wasn't going to tell us anything new, so we scheduled an angiogram (actually looking at my arteries from the inside with a camera) to get a clear picture.

Is the plan working?

My wife and I figured that, according to my plan of eating well and exercising every day, I was catching a small problem before it got to be a big one. Boy was I wrong. Exercising every day meant that a small problem was no problem for me until it *became* a big problem. The diagnosis: 3 severely clogged arteries... again! My treatment options: at least 4 more stents or cardiac bypass (open-heart) surgery. Yeah, that's what you want to have to decide with 2 kids in college.

The decision was actually very easy. I can vividly remember being in the hospital and being completely aware of what was happening. I reflected on the fact that both of my parents had similar surgery and had gone on to, and still are, living good lives. I reflected on the situation and my first thought, which I verbalized to my wife, was: *"We have grandchildren who aren't even a thought yet that we have to be around to spoil"*. That's because I've heard that becoming a grandparent is your reward for not killing your children!

As I write this it's over 4 years since my triple bypass surgery. It's been quite a few years. Deciding to have bypass surgery has, once again, changed my perspective on everyday things. Other decisions have become a lot easier. You've heard the expression *"Don't sweat the small stuff"* and *"It's all small stuff"*, well, I wholeheartedly agree. I live that every day.

Chapter 23
What I did for my birthday

I had a special, milestone birthday the summer after my bypass surgery. I had been talking about what I was going to do for this birthday for a long time. It was a perpetual item on my *bucket list*. I mentioned it to a college friend and he said that he had the same "Someday Isle" idea, but no one to do it with him. So we agreed to do it together. Our wives came to support us and his wife decided to join us when we got there.

So the week of my birthday, from 13,500 feet, the three of us stepped out of a perfectly good airplane and went skydiving. It surprised me that I had no trepidation when it was my turn to go. I just walked up to the door with my tandem buddy, Serge, and we stepped out. Six or seven minutes later we were on the ground and we each have photos and videos to prove it. If you and I are Facebook friends you can see the photos and video on my page: (facebook.com/alanberg1).

Would I do it again? Yes. Do I have a burning desire to do it again now? No. I was able to cross that one off my bucket list so don't *have* to do it again, but I would. Instead, my wife and I are thinking that hot-air ballooning would be nice. We've heard that Santa Fe, New Mexico is the place to go, so we put it on our joint bucket list. Stay tuned.

Chapter 24
A new chapter, a new challenge

As I was writing this book the company, where I had worked for over 11 years, decided it was time for us to part ways. My first thought was that this is not an ideal time for this to happen. My younger son was still in college, we had two houses (one which we rented out when it didn't sell during the housing bust), two mortgages, and so on. This wasn't an ideal time for this to happen.

I had already thought about what I would do if I didn't work for that company as there had been chatter on financial message boards, blogs and articles over the years, about it being a possible take-over target. If that happened I could easily find myself being shown the door, as so often happens with a merger/take-over. What gave me comfort was knowing that I knew what I'd like to do. I'd want to continue speaking, writing and working with small and medium-sized businesses around the country. The only difference was that I would no longer be under the umbrella of that company; I would be my own brand.

Know your personal brand

What I had recently started to realize was that my personal brand had already been established in the hearts and minds of my audience. They felt connected to me, personally, not because I worked for that company. My friends tell me that my personal brand has been established for quite some time, but I had no reason to see it. I had been at this company for a long time and was proud to be there while it was the leader in its field. The CEO had once told me that this was the last company I would ever have to work for. I took that as a compliment and to mean that I would retire from that company. I guess that if you don't count me working for my own company, he was right! It wasn't how I had thought it would be, but that's the reality of life. Take every day as it comes. I like to say that I live for today while planning for tomorrow.

There's never an ideal time

So while this was not the ideal time for this to happen, I realized that there will never be an ideal time. There will always be some reason *not* to make the leap; some self-imposed roadblock holding me back. It would have been nice to have had a running head start, instead of a shove.

I told my wife that someday we're going to look back at this and see that this was a most wonderful opportunity. Today's not that day, but someday (I write this with tongue in cheek and a smile on my face). We're both very excited at the prospects and opportunities ahead. I prefer to think of it that they paid me to start the business I'm supposed to be doing. I was talking with a friend of mine and he said I was taking a very *"Alan Berg view"* of this and making lemonade out of lemons.

Thanks for your support

I'm touched by the incredible phone calls, emails and notes I've been getting saying how I've taught people, mentored them and touched them, both personally as well as professionally. I believe that ultimately people judge you not by what you say you're going to do, rather by what you do and how you make people feel along the way. I've often said that if you don't like me when I'm on stage, you won't like me at the dinner table, at the bar or on the golf course. There's only one me and I bring him wherever I go. There's no game-face. There's no mask. There's just me.

I recall hearing that if you're interviewing someone to come work for you, or maybe considering dating someone, see how they treat the waiter or waitress at a restaurant. If they're nice to you, but not so nice to the server, they're probably putting on their game-face for you. Their true colors are showing in how they treat the wait staff. If you're like me, you prefer dealing with people who are truly genuine. I find it exhausting trying to turn on and off different facades. It's so much easier to just have one, the real one.

Two years and counting

It's been just over two years now and I'm having the time of my life. I'm traveling to places I'd probably never have seen, getting to meet wonderful, caring people and it's a blast. The fact that I get to help so many people reach higher and higher, whether it's a better website or a better attitude, makes it all worthwhile.

Chapter 25
The journey continues

I'd like to believe that I'm done with my cardiac issues forever, but as I said early in this book, I'm a realist. I do have full confidence that whatever comes my way I'll be able to stay one step ahead of it. That said, I refuse to be defined by the history of my health. I want people to see me first as a good person; a good family man; someone who has knowledge and passion to share with people like you. That's my attitude and my choice, and I'm sticking with it. It has served me well so far.

Life is full of stories. Some surprise us, some shock us and some inspire us. What are you waiting for? What is it that you want to do that you've putting off? What is the "house" you're trying to paint (literally or metaphorically)?

Are you thinking of expanding your business? Are you thinking of raising your prices? Are you thinking of starting a diet or exercise program? Are you thinking of writing a book? Are you thinking of going skydiving? What's your Someday Isle?

Do you have the strength and courage to take at least one new step today towards achieving those dreams? I'll bet that you do.

Can you strive to become the positive voice that others want to be around? Yes, you can. After all, it's your attitude and your choice. I have faith that you'll choose wisely.

Thanks for investing your time with me and this book. Please share your stories of success with me on my website **www.AlanBerg.com,** or directly, through email at **YourAttitude@AlanBerg.com**

From The Author

Who is Alan Berg? If I had to answer this in one sentence I'd say "I'm a Suburban Renaissance Man". I'm a husband, father, son, brother, friend, speaker, author, salesman, marketer, musician, handyman, consultant, teacher and all-around nice guy. I'm passionate about my family and my work. I love being creative and working with my hands as well as my mind. That's one of the reasons there's a wrench in my personal logo.

I've worked in sales, marketing and sales management for over 25 years, over 20 in wedding media. I spent 11 years at The Knot (at the time the largest, busiest wedding media site in the world), most as Vice President of Sales and Vice President of The Knot Market Intelligence. I'm a professional speaker and proud member of the National Speakers Association, the leading organization for professional speakers, where I've been honored to present as well as play keyboard in the NSA All-Star Band.

I revel in the success of others and truly believe that your success will lead to more success for me and for everyone. I believe that when you give first you'll get more than you could have ever asked for in return. I also believe in living for today, while planning for tomorrow. I know that this information can help you, as it has for so many others, and I appreciate you picking up my book. I look forward to hearing how you've implemented these ideas.

Thank you.

Please post your thoughts about this book on my site at **www.ReviewMyBook.net**

In addition to writing books and articles I have the privilege of traveling around the country, and internationally, performing keynote addresses and workshops, as well as doing in-house trainings. If you'd like to have me speak for your company, conference, group or association, train your sales and customer support teams or to have me review your website or help you with consulting or coaching services, please contact me:

- email: **YourAttitude@AlanBerg.com**
- visit: **www.AlanBerg.com**
- call: **732.422.6362**
- international: **001 732 422 6362**

About The Author

Alan Berg is fluent in the language of business. He's been in marketing, sales and sales management for over 20 years, working with businesses of all sizes, many in the wedding and event industry. Before striking out on his own as a business consultant, author and professional speaker, he served as Vice President of Sales and The Knot Market Intelligence at **The Knot** (now the XO Group), the leading life stage media company. In additional to his speaking and consulting he also serves as a consultant and Education Guru for **WeddingWire**, the leading wedding technology company, doing webinars, live presentations, writing articles and more.

He's able to help new businesses and solopreneurs, as well as established players and corporations, understand and achieve their goals. Alan understands business as he's owned several of his own, including publishing two wedding magazines. He understands what it's like to make payroll, do the books, do collections, apply for a loan and manage/hire/fire/train employees. He knows what you're going through and feels your pain.

Through his extensive experience, speaking and consulting domestically and internationally, Alan understands that the needs of wedding businesses are not that different from the needs of all businesses. You all want to find, capture and retain customers. If you're reading this book you want actionable content, not exhaustive homework and that's what you'll get. Alan purposely made this book short so you can get to the action part faster. Get started now on your journey to greater success.

Share Alan's unique inspirational, actionable content

If you'd like to have Alan speak for your company, conference, group or association, to thank your key partners for their referrals, for bulk copies of this book to inspire your team or members, and to find out about his website review and consulting services for your business, large or small (yes, even if you're the only employee), contact Alan:
- email: **YourAttitude@AlanBerg.com**
- visit: **www.AlanBerg.com**
- call: **732.422.6362**
- international: **001 732 422 6362**

"Yours was the best seminar that I attended at Wedding MBA. I get bored listening to most people talk for more than 10 minutes, but you kept it interesting and me engaged."
Lance Morris, Spokane, WA

◇ ◻ ◻ ◻ ◇

"Alan Berg is skilled speaker. He can take any topic and make it dynamic. He is among the highest ranked speakers year after year at the Wedding MBA. Alan is able to take technical subject matter and make it interesting. *I have yet to see Alan Berg give a speech that is anything but exceptional! We recommend Alan without reservation."*
Shannon Underwood, Scottsdale, AZ

◇ ◻ ◻ ◻ ◇

"I heard Alan speak at on two different occasions... both times he left me motivated, intrigued, and thinking about ways to improve my business. Things I may think I am doing right, he made me look back to see ways to better improve upon. I've already implemented some things I have learned and seen a change in production. Would love to hear him speak again."
Katrina McCullum, Jacksonville, FL

◇ ◻ ◻ ◻ ◇

"Alan is one of the few speakers that I will make time to see over and over. He also is the only speaker that gets a standing ovation. Alan understands and solves problems and always has fresh new ideas."
Sal Richetti, Pittsburgh, PA

Forward

For those who don't know, I have a Facebook page, I take pictures of beautiful old buildings and tell their stories. Some are happy and some are sad, but they all deserve to be remembered. American history is a patch work of small local histories that have combined to form our great country. If a quilt starts missing some of the patches it is made of, it stops being a quilt and becomes a raggedy blanket. Too often schools have only taught what is required for standardized testing, and within a few generations local history is forgotten by most, remembered only by historians and those directly affected.

Due to local social and economic issues, I chose Hood in the Woods as my name. I live in southwest Virginia, right next to south West Virginia. Lots of small towns whose economy is based on one industry, and as the industry declines so does the town. Many of my posts have gone viral. Histories of small forgotten towns and pictures of beautiful houses. In the age of people being offended, no one has ever been offended by a picture of their house of pictures of their town appearing on a page called Hood in the Woods. You don't have to understand the name, others do.

This area has always had a lot agriculture. At first it was slaves and plantations. During the Civil War West Virginia seceded from Virginia. 20 years later company towns covered the region.

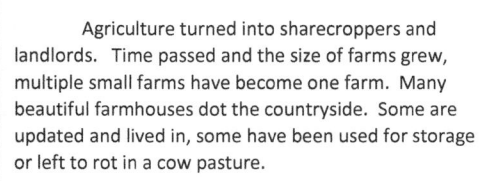

Agriculture turned into sharecroppers and landlords. Time passed and the size of farms grew, multiple small farms have become one farm. Many beautiful farmhouses dot the countryside. Some are updated and lived in, some have been used for storage or left to rot in a cow pasture.

Find me at The Real hood in the woods on facebook. Hood in the woods on Youtube. Abandoned_in_Appalachia on Instagram.